Coming Out of My Shell

Poetry From the Soul

By

Calvin Butler

authorHOUSE™

1663 LIBERTY DRIVE, SUITE 200
BLOOMINGTON, INDIANA 47403
(800) 839-8640
WWW.AUTHORHOUSE.COM

First published by AuthorHouse 04/07/05

ISBN: 1-4208-0973-3 (sc)
ISBN: 1-4208-0972-5 (dj)

Printed in the United States of America
Bloomington, Indiana

This book is printed on acid-free paper.

I would like to thank family and friends who have supported and encouraged me for many years to have my poems published. My church family, Mt. Canaan Baptist, Mattie Tanks Springs, Debra Robinson and Beatrice Toomer have all been very inspirational to me. Thanks to everyone for their encouraging words.

Editorial Director:	Betty Butler
Project Editor:	Calvin Butler
Creative Manager:	Calvin Butler
Book Cover design:	Allegra Print & Imaging (Bartley S. Harper)
Book Cover photographs:	M's Finest Photography (Wesley Hightower)
Book Sketches:	Beth Wade (Art teacher/Strom Thurmond High School)
	Beatrice Toomer (Retired New York Postal Employee)
Computer Designs/Layout:	Jason Wellband

Dedication

This book is dedicated to my wife, Betty; Darold, my son; Junetta, my daughter-in-law; Jayden, my grandson; Darrien, my granddaughter; Kimberly Strickland, goddaughter; friends, Debra Robinson, Ethel Robinson, Ella Young, mother-in-law, and Robert Lee Young, brother-in-law.

Calvin Butler

Table of Contents

Section One: Love Poems

A Flower in my Heart for our Love

I met Betty long ago
Not knowing whether she was friend or foe
What happened? I just don't know,
But there's a flower in my heart for our love.

This flower will last through the duration of time
This flower is in symmetry, rhythm and rhyme
This flower will be forever sublime
There's a flower in my heart for our love.

I like the way she stays so calm and composed.
Her fragrance is sweeter than the sweetest rose
And my love for her just grows and grows
There's a flower in my heart for our love.

Her prestige makes me feel like
A happy chum
And I will always dance to the beat
Of her melodious drum
I hope you understand where I am coming from,
There's a flower in my heart for our love.

Betty and I share a special kind of love
The kind that descended from heaven above
When I'm depressed, God and Betty are my only cove.
There's a flower in my heart for our love.

This flower is the color of evergreen
The most beautiful flower I've ever seen.
Try to picture in your mind's eye what I mean
There's a flower in my heart for our love.

2-25-98

Calvin Butler

Bewitching Love

One day I met a woman
She was super fine.
She was very warm and human
She started playing with my mind.

She uttered an incantation
And then she cast a spell
That started our relation
And in love with her I fell.

Even though we are apart
She never leaves my mind
I could have loved her from the start
I was easily inclined.

At her I took a look,
Then I took a glance.
She is as beautiful as a poetry book
That's written about romance.

She is as stubborn as a mule.
She can withstand the test of time,
But for her I will be a fool,
As long as poetry rhymes.

6-5-64

Confidant

You're my lover, my confidant
My companion and my friend.
Intimately you touched me,
Taking me where I've never been.
To a place of perfection,
Where everything is in symmetry,
And in you I found affection,
Happiness and love in ecstasy.
I met you at the right time.
You're kind and unconceited.
Now my life is sublime,
You're everything I needed.
Yes, you are my confidant
In you, I can confide.
You're everything I could ever want,
And we have nothing to hide.

12-5-78

For the Fun of It

Honey, I love you and I won't ever quit.
I am going to take care of you "for the fun of it."
When I met you, you were so sweet and kind,
I could not forget I wanted you to be mine.

Then we dated for a little while
I was so elated over your beautiful smile.
Then we married and we had a son.
That is the best thing that has happened to me
Since I've been born.

I am going to love him and never quit,
And take care of him "for the fun of it."
I know sometimes our lives are filled with gloom,
But don't leave me, just sleep in the other room.
I won't do anything that I think unwise.
If we argue, we can always compromise.

I can love you and not ever quit,
And take care of you "for the fun of it."
I know sometimes we don't see eye to eye.
If you must leave, don't leave for another guy
Then I can love you with a love I won't regret
And take care of you "for the fun of it."

1-8-75

If I Were a Master Key

If I were a master key
I would open the door to your mind,
Then curious I would never more be
But astonished at what I would find.

If I were a master key
I would unlock the door to your heart.
Then all your love would belong to me
Until death when we depart.

3-19-75

Calvin Butler

If Your Love was Measured in Quantity

If your love was measured in quantity,
There'd be no limit to your love for me.
If you could be judged by your tender touch,
Your selfish ways wouldn't mean half as much.

If I could count your love for me.
It would be more than the number system could ever be.
You have everything a guy could ever long for.
I'd be a fool to ask for anything more.

If I could spell your love my dear
My vocabulary would have to reach a far and near
Your love for me is the very best,
And I'm not going to settle for anything less.

If your love was measured in inches and feet,
Every inch of your love, would be so very sweet.
I am so very fond of your loving me so much,
I hope I never loose my magic touch.

2-3-69

I'm Back in the Rat Race Again

When I got your letter the other day,
I was about to go astray.
My mind was so vexed with sin,
But the inspirational things you had to say
Made me feel better in every way.
Now I'm back in the rat race again.

I was feeling down and out
Had a lot to worry about.
Loneliness was my only friend,
But the sweet things you unfolded,
Was more precious than silver or gold.
Put me back in the rat race again.

I was feeling so discontented,
Like my "get up and go" had got up and went.
But I have outwitted the best of men,
I find it shocking to say,
That all strength had gone away.
You put me back in the rat race again.

Various things had me worried a lot.
I pay my bills with the money I've got.
I can't depend on my closet kin.
Good luck fell upon me that day.
You drove all my troubles away.
Now, I'm back in the rat race again.

I was feeling chained and bound,
Couldn't find a friend around.
But my mind was changed so hurriedly,
By the sweet things you said to me.
You put me back in the rat race again.

11-8-68

Laughter

Laughter is when
I feel good within
Just for a minute.
I feel laughter because you're my wife
And I'll feel laughter all my life
As long as you're in it.

Even though I never smile
But every once in a while
I am filled with laughter.
And you'll always have my heart
Even if we are apart
Now and ---- after

Laughter is an incoherent word
That's very often heard
In times of pleasure.
And no one could ever be
As close as you are to me
My greatest treasure.

2-20-88

Calvin Butler

My Love is an Interchangeable Thing

My love is like a faucet
I can turn it off and on,
My love is like a dependent clause
That can not stand alone.

My love is like a flower
That blooms in the spring.
I can change my love every hour
It's an interchangeable thing.

My love is like the leaves
That in the autumn falls.
My love is like beautiful trees,
The most beautiful of all.

My love is like the mocking bird
And the different songs it sings.
My love is an indescribable word,
And interchangeable thing.

My love is sweet as honey
But like the bee it stings.
Do you think it's funny?
It's an interchangeable thing.

3-24-70

Nothingness

Betty, I miss you in the utmost degree
Oh, how I wish I had you here with me
Girl, you really left me in distress
My life is filled with nothingness.

You said absence makes the heart grows fonder
Well, I'm going to try and withstand the test.
Since you've been gone, all I do is wonder.
My life is filled with nothingness.

When you were home,
I didn't have the urge to roam,
I was overwhelmed by your sweet caress!
But since you left,
I haven't been myself,
My life is filled with nothingness.

I don't want you to think I'm a nag,
Nor to think I'm just a pest.
But you left me with an empty bag.
My life is filled with nothingness.

Sometimes I wonder if you're true,
And are you the girl that I possess.
You should be if you want our love to endure.
My life is filled with nothingness.

Betty, you mean the most to me.
You are the key to my success.
In your arms is where I want to be,
Then my life wouldn't be filled with nothingness.

8-29-69

In 1968 Betty went to college and feelings of emptiness filled my life
because we were such close friends. Because of her absence, I was
inspired to write "Nothingness.".

Thank You For Sharing My Life With Me

You took the time to get to know me
When no one else ever did.
You always found my inhibitions
I thought I had so deeply hid.

You took me to a place in affection
No one else ever could
And in every bad situation
You always see some good.

You are a very positive person
With a lot of magnetic pull.
When I see a glass half empty,
You see the glass half full.

If I should die today or tonight
It really has been a blast.
So superstar keep shinning bright
In the future like in the past.

I think you are the most kind,
And sensitive person on this planet earth,
And when it comes to love and compassion,
You are the one that gave it birth.

Thank you for sharing my life with me
It has really been a blast.
I know through death and infinity
Our love will forever last!

11-23-95

When We Embrace

When we embrace I want to be
Head to head, eyes to eyes, neck to neck
Shoulders to shoulders, stomach to stomach
Navel to navel, don't make no mistake.

When we embrace, I want to be face to face
Nose to nose, knees to knees, waist to waist
Arms to arms, ankles to ankles, toes to toes
Feet to feet and elbows to elbows.

Don't turn away and hug me from the side
That's not my groove, that's not my glide.
When we embrace, I want to be mouth to mouth
Cheek to cheek and chin to chin.

So when you hug me once
You'll want to hug me again.
When we embrace, I want to be eyes to eyes
Nose to nose, thighs to thighs.

Don't turn away and embrace me from the side
That's not my modus operandi, not my glide.
If you want to embrace me from the side
Please don't, I'll tell you what I really want.

I want to be mouth to mouth, nose to nose
Stomach to stomach, face to face
Cheek to cheek, legs to legs
Toes to toes and waist to waist.
Then I can give you a feeling
That will send you reeling through time and space!

8-9-02

Section Two: Inner Turmoil

Calvin Butler

A Person Within a Person

I'm a person within a person
Just struggling to be free
In a prison within a prison
Embedded deep inside of me.
Trapped between mixed emotions
Only fate holds the key.
A person within a person
Just struggling to be free.

I have a dream within a dream
Larger than a sea within a sea
With aspirations that seem
To want equality.
A person within a person
Just struggling to be free.
In a prison within a prison
Embedded deep inside of me.

7-10-94

A Zero Has No Value By Itself

Betty, without you in my life
My life would be like a zero
But having you for my wife
I feel like I am a hero.

You see I can have the world
And all of its pelf
But a zero has no value
by itself.

You can use a zero with other numbers
To give it great worth
With you in my life, Betty
I am the happiest man on earth.

But without you in my life
There would be no loving or living left
Because a zero has
No value by itself.

The two of us together will always
Make beautiful clef
But a zero has
No value by itself.

When you got sick, Betty
I thought I was going to have
To put my love on the shelf
Because a zero has no value by itself.

I thought for a while
That all my dreams were cleft
Because a zero has no
value by itself.

I am going to keep on loving you
While there's some loving and living left
Because this zero
Has no value by itself.

Betty, the good news from the doctor
Really gave me mirth
I feel like I'm the happiest
Man on earth.
And I am going to continue loving you
Beyond height, width and depth
Because a zero has
No value by itself.

7-25-02

My wife has survived cancer for over fourteen years. Because of a
similar scare of this disease with her, I pondered what my life would be
like without her, resulting in this poem.

If Only We Can Laugh

The journey through life
Sometimes is very lonely,
But remember dear wife
I will always love you only.

Sometimes our hearts
Seem to be broken in half
Our loneliness will depart
If we can only laugh.

We need something to break our pensive mood
When we are in the agony of solitude.
Just think of something that's very funny
Laugh then you'll feel better, honey.

Sometimes we feel
With people we should mingle,
But when they get what they want
Then they no longer linger.

A pseudo friend
We can find a plenty,
But a genuine friend
We're fortunate if we find any.

11-25-93

I'm not a Forest, I'm a Tree

When people look at me
They don't see what they really should see
Because I'm not a forest,
I'm a tree!

People say all men are alike
I don't see how that could possibly be
Because I'm not a forest,
I'm a tree!

I'm as different from other people
As an elbow is from a knee
I'm not a forest,
I'm a tree!

They could open the door to my heart,
If only they had the right key.
You see, I'm not a forest,
I'm a tree!

Even though I'm part of the human race
I have my own individuality
I am not a forest,
I am a tree!

If my countenance is unpleasant
My inner beauty is far deeper
Than the human eye can see.
I am not a forest but a tree.

I'm as different from other people
As a metaphor is from a simile.
I'm not a forest,
I'm a tree!

I will stand for what is right
If I have to stand individually,
I'm not a forest, I'm a tree.

I'm as different from other people
As two is from three
I'm not a forest, I'm a tree.

It may seem like I'm fighting a losing battle
But the righteous will win inevitably
I'm not a forest,
I'm a tree.

I am only a constituent
Of the whole anatomy
I'm not a forest,
I am a tree!

If you must judge me
Judge me for my merits and my personality
I'm not a forest,
I'm a tree!

When people learn to accept people
For who they are, and not who they should be
Then they won't be a forest
They'll be a tree!

12-23-01

In the Pot About to Stew

I'm out on a limb
And I'm going down.
I thought I could swim,
But I am about to drown.

.

I have committed no crimes
Honey, I have been true.
I've been down two times
Tell me what must I do?

I'm in the pot
I'm about to stew.
Will I lose a lot,
If I fall for you?

I have been playing around
Just to have some fun.
But I let my guard down,
And you knocked a homerun.

It's worse than a cold
It's worse than the flu.
It's out of control.
Tell me what can I do?

Your grip is stronger
Than crazy glue.
I can't hold out much longer,
Tell me what must I do?

The fire is hot
Wonder will I subdue
I'm in the pot
And about to stew.

5-29-68

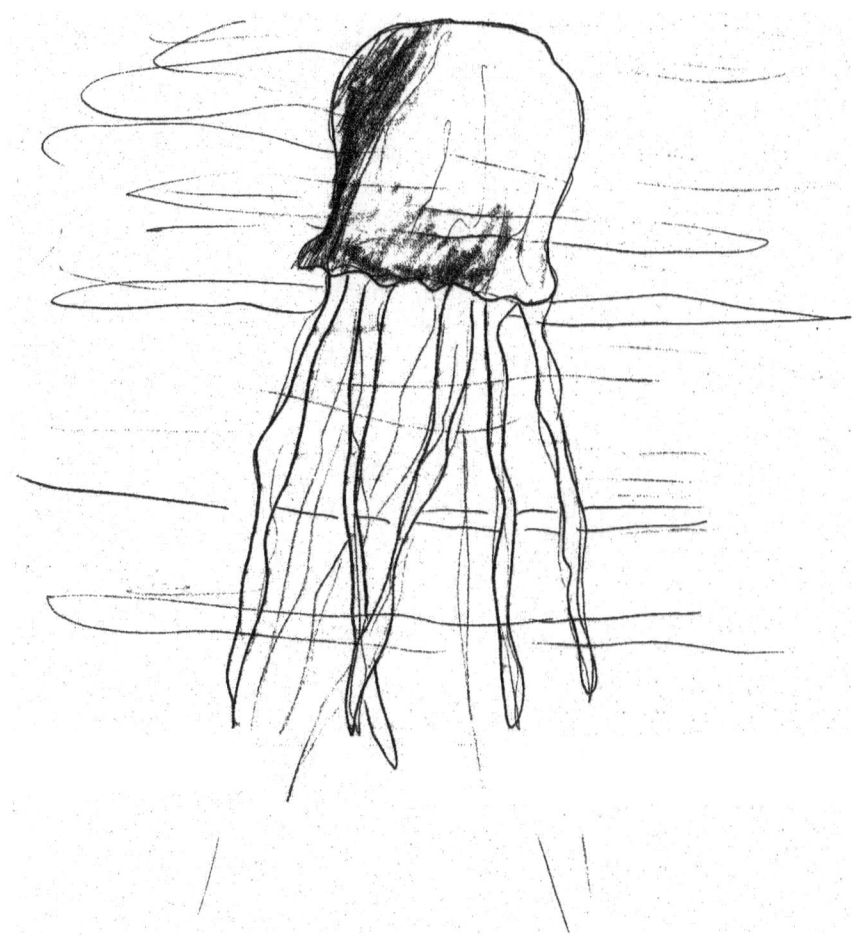

Jellyfish

Some people are like the jellyfish.
We are not, but sometimes I wish
Because if we were, then we could go
Whatever way the stream would flow.

Into the ocean, into the sea,
The problems in life wouldn't bother me.
Into the rivers, into the brooks,
Not pausing at life's second look.

Leisure time would be my favorite dish,
If I were like the Jellyfish,
Or like the vulture flying high,
Above the earth, under the sky,

No burdens on his back to bear,
Just sailing freely through the air.
Just sailing freely to and fro
Depending on the wind to blow,
Without a gesture or a wish,
It's somewhat like the Jellyfish.

7-15-99

My Poetry

My poetry is like a river,
Running perpetually in my head.
And I will keep writing forever,
Until everything is said.

My poetry is like a fire burning,
Without consuming it's energy.
My poetry is a desire yearning,
Reaching for its destiny.

My poetry is more than a phrase or a thought.
My poetry is more than just notions.
My feelings can't be sold or bought,
They stem from real emotions.

Can you get into my poetry?
If you can get into my poetry,
Then you can get into me,
Because my poetry is the poet
And I am the poetry.

11-3-99

Neutral

I am a color without a color
I have a heart without a care
I am a person without a purpose
I'm not going anywhere.

I blend with colors many,
But only compatible to a few.
A true friend I don't have any,
Well, maybe one or two.

If you are wondering why I am neutral
Or think I don't make any sense,
Well, I've found that being neutral
Is my only self-defense.

You see by being neutral,
I am transparent, crystal clear.
Then people don't know they hurt me,
And the pain won't be so severe.

But I am beauty, hidden beauty.
I'm really something to behold.
I'm a child in a man's body,
Growing young instead of old.

I am a diamond in the rough.
I'm not cheap simulated glass.
I have a mind with a memory,
Of my horrid childhood past.

I am adventurous, explore me.
I am a story that's never been told.
If you continue to follow the rainbow,
Pretty soon you'll find the gold.

I am a book without a story.
I am an actor without a play.
Maybe between here and glory,
I might find myself one day.

6-9-96

Never a Name, Just a Number

When you play life's game
It will cause you to tumble,
That's why I'm never a name,
But always a number.

When I'm running a touchdown
Don't cause me to fumble,
Because I'm never a name,
But always a number.

I don't ever complain
Nor do I grumble.
I am never a name,
But always a number.

I try to walk circumspectly
But sometimes I stumble,
Because I'm never a name,
But always a number.

The reason why I have humility,
And I am humble.
I am never a name,
But always a number.

9-11-03

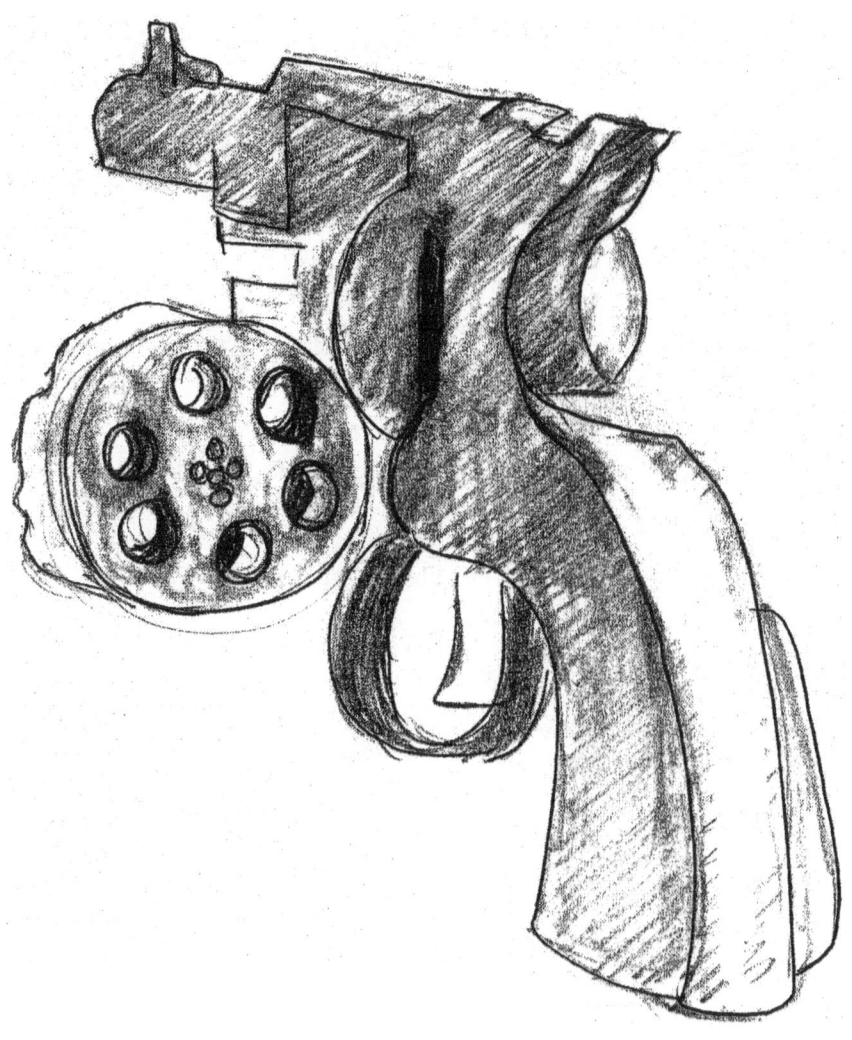

Russian Roulette

Once upon a time
When I was a kid.
I did something
No one would suspect I did.

We played a game
We made a bet.
The game was called
Russian roulette.

I was about eleven years old,
And so I did what I was told.
My brother Thomas said
"Snap this gun upside your head."

We played a game
I now regret.
The game was called
Russian roulette.

Thomas and I
Took our stance,
And then we played
That game of chance.

We would put one bullet
In the gun,
Spin the cylinder,
And snap it just for fun.

Our odds were six to one
Of being killed by the gun.
It's a wonder I'm not dead.
I snapped a gun up side my head.

We wanted to see
Who was afraid,
When we snapped the gun
Beside our head.

I don't know,
But I contend,
That God wasn't ready
For me then.

I know now without a doubt,
And it's not a bet.
When you play with God,
You are playing Russian roulette.

9-9-03

The Boy The World Forgot

He never had a life as a boy.
I am lying not.
He never had a friend or a toy.
The boy the world forgot.

He would stand on life's shore,
Watching people go, go plotting up a plot,
Through writ and wrought they would leave him out.
The boy the world forgot.

He met many girls with their hair in curls.
He loved them, they loved him not.
They took his heart, tore it apart.
The boy the world forgot.

Now, he's a man, he doesn't understand
What life is all about.
He lives his life in a wonderland,
The man the world forgot.

6-1-70

Calvin Butler

The Brotherhood of Man

I believe in the brotherhood of man
I am an aquarian if you understand
And my colors shine.
I can be led but I cannot be driven
I am as far ahead as the earth is from heaven
Of the other signs.

Peace and harmony is my by-word.
I'm out to change anything
That I think is absurd.
For I believe one man can bring about a change.
I'm friendly to lots of people, but a friend to a few
Faithful and loyal, devoted and true.
Some people may think that I am strange

Because they find it hard to pin me down.
But I am creative, prolific, and I'm profound.
I can see light years in the future.
But even with my ability to dream and think creatively
Sometimes I need the feminine nurture.

True Color

I thought you were my friend and scholar.
I would have given you my last dollar,
Acting cool like you are all mellow,
But your true color is the color of yellow.

You don't know what I am about.
When under pressure, you cop out.
Well, I will tell you something big fellow.
Your true color is the color of yellow.

I would have given you my last dime
And stood by you time after time
And shielded you as if I were an umbrella,
But your true color is the color of yellow.

Sometimes you have to take a stand.
Just to prove that you are a man.
You remind me of a woman named Stella.
Her true color was the color of yellow.

You can't stand on both sides of a fence.
Don't live in fear but reverence.
If someone do me wrong, I stand and bellow,
My true color is not the color of yellow.

9-14-03

Section Three: Tributes

A Tribute to Josephine

Requiem for a Queen

When I was born, she was fourteen
My elder sister Josephine.
She was like no other.
I loved her like a sister,
I loved her like a mother.
She was so kind, she wasn't mean,
And maybe her life wasn't squeaky clean,
But I don't think she was so bad,
She did the best she could with what she had.
She taught me what survival means,
That's why I'm writing this requiem for a queen.
She always had the power to forgive,
And she wasn't afraid of dying,
Because she knew how to live.
Even though I never cried,
I felt so empty inside
The day my sister Josephine died.
She left a legacy behind,
For us to treat each other kind.
She will forever remain in my heart
And in my mind.

4-7-03

An Ode to Jessie

After the Rain

After the rain
Flowers bloom
And life is sustained.
But after the pain
Only "time " will smooth
The jagged edges again.

Life is like a seed
That the farmer sows.
It has to be planted indeed
Before a new crop can grow.

Jessie planted a seed.
He planted it for the Lord.
A good thought, a kind seed,
Was the kind of seed he sowed.

In everyone's life
A little rain must fall.
But through struggle and strife
The sun will shine through it all.

God doesn't make mistakes.
He is just fulfilling His quest.
So He called Jessie to heaven
So he could be His guest.

An Ode to my Mother

I loved you when you were young and pretty,
And needless shall I say.
I love you now and not out of pity
Because you're old and gray.

Whenever I needed a friend
You always were the best
You stuck by me until the end
To that I can attest.

Through the corridors of time, you've always given
Your tender love and care
And if there's but one crown in heaven
I know that crown you'll wear.

So eventhough we have to depart
Forever you'll live inside my heart.
The emptiness you've left behind
Mere words cannot express.
But I hope in life's end you'll find
Eternal happiness.

An Ode to Rev. George L. Brightharp

Just to mention his name
Makes me somewhat tense.
He is the Poet Laurete of intelligence.
A great leader, philosopher, an educator,
A preacher, businessman, and an orator.
But Rev. Brightharp is truly
A man of God first
His ministry is like water in a desert
To a man dying of thirst.
But what does Rev. Brightharp's ministry means to me
Let me try to explain:
It's like the Las Vegas heat
Or the California rain.
It's like watching the sun set
On an ocean or a sea.
His ministry means a lot to the church,
And it means a lot to me.
His spiritual charisma is like a malignant tumor,
He has razor sharp incisive wit, and a good sense of humor.
But what does his ministry means to me,
Let me try to explain, it's like medicine from a doctor
That soothes excruciating pain.
Each time I hear his sermons
They are always refreshing and new.
It's like walking barefooted
In the misty morning dew.

One more thing I want to say about Rev. Brightharp
It's sad, but it's true.
If you mess around and die,
Ole Rev. will bury you!

1-24-00

An Ode to Uncle Nat

He was like a brother to us, a precious gem
Our only Uncle Nat.
And I would gladly tip my hat to him
But I don't wear a hat.

He came to comfort the family
And to see our brother Grant,
But then he left in the same chariot
That my God had sent.

No one knows where death is
Or what's around the bend,
But death is a new beginning,
Death is not the end.

I really believe he knew the Lord
He always had a vision
And so he left in such sweet accord
But that was God's decision.

3-25-85

Cheer Up, God Will Mend Your Heart

Cheer up young Lady, cheer up.
Don't mope your life away.
I know you both are wise, so you must realize
That there is a brighter day.

Cheer up young man, cheer up.
Please don't ever fall apart.
Even though sorrow has filled your cup,
The Lord can mend your heart.

She was a lady with so much grace.
Even though her youth wasn't spent.
I know nothing will ever take her place,
Because she made you both so content.

Now she is somewhere around God's throne,
With the angels and the heavenly host.
So all the love you all might have known,
Jesus Christ loves her the most.

7-20-72

Darrien

Excuse me while I stand and stare
At your beautiful skin and cold, dark hair.
As my wife held her, Jayden smiled,
Then I saw love in the eyes of a child.

Darrien is about as wide as my hand.
Her complexion a lighter shade of tan
But she really makes our heart glad
Because she is the daughter we never had.

When I held her in my arms, she made my heart smile.
Then suddenly I felt somewhat infantile.
God help us to raise her in admonition and grace
Until we leave here for a better place.

She was sleeping, then she opened her eyes wide.
God help us to take care of her, for she is our pride.
I kept thinking how she made our hearts glad
Because she is the daughter we never had.

My wife gave her a bottle of milk
And wrapped her in a cover of silk.
Watching her made our hearts feel glad
Because she is the daughter we never had.

11-22-03

Family and Friends' Day

I am happy to be a part of this church family.
I am filled with joy and bliss
Because when two or three people meet in the
Name of Jesus, God is always in the midst.

In order to have a successful church family
We must exemplify humility and love.
These are some of the attributes Jesus depicted
When he descended from heaven above.

We must have a humble spirit
And always be willing to forgive,
Then we won't be afraid of dying
Because we will know how to live.

We must condescend to the lowly
And always be willing to serve
Then God will pour out his blessings
More than we could ever deserve.

We must always sow good seeds,
And God will bless us our whole life long,
And we must always do kind deeds,
Then God's love will keep us strong.

We can find strength if we stick together,
And we must not do each other wrong.
Then we can control our whole body,
If we learn to tame our tongue.

In our times of trials and tribulations,
Let's never forget to pray.
When it seems we have no way out,
God will always make a way.

Let's let our love be like a circle.
A circle doesn't ever end.
Let's never stop loving our family and friends,
Because a quitter doesn't ever win.

If you don't remember everything I have said,
I hope you remember one thing I say,
God blesses the family and friends
Who never forget to pray.

9-12-02

In the Renaissance of Time

A Tribute to Jayden

My wife and I went to a place
So peaceful and sublime,
And I saw myself living
In the renaissance of time.

In a second generation
A little boy was born,
And by reincarnation
My second life was shown.

It made me so happy.
I heard beautiful bells chime,
When I saw myself living
In the renaissance of time.

He has his mother's beauty,
And he has his father's charm.
And I felt so elated,
When I held him in my arms.

As my wife talked to our baby,
All I could do was mime.
When I saw myself living,
In the renaissance of time.

At first he opened his eyes,
And then he started to smile.
Then I paused for a minute,
To reminisce for a while.

Like a meter in poetry,
And lyrics in a song,
A feeling came over me,
That was very strong.

I took a walk down memory lane,
All the way back to my prime,
When I saw myself living,
In the renaissance of time.

I would be a trillionaire,
If I had a nickel or a dime,
For the times I thought about living
In the renaissance of time.

He was somewhat little,
Not much wider than my hand,
But I'll tell you something Jayden,
I'll always be your greatest fan.

Let's all take Jayden by his hand,
God please control his mind.
Help him live to see himself living,
In the renaissance of time.

4-19-02

Calvin Butler

On the Floor, Looking Under the Door

Who is this that's always on the floor
Looking under the door?
Who is this? The badder he is
I love him more.

Who is this who is never in sad array or gloom?
Who is this who never sleeps in the bed in his room?
Who is this who is always tumbling over his head,
Always crying when it's time to go to bed?

Who is this who is always leaving his toys on the floor?
When we eat, he asks for more.
Who is it who walks like a pimp, so cool
That's going to American Creative School?

Jacob Lawrence
Artist

Dean
Dixon
Symphony
Conductor

Phillis Wheatley
Poet

Some Famous Figures in Black History

Jesse Owens set records in the hundred yard dash.
Records were set and broken in tennis by Arthur Ashe.
Harriet Tubman led slaves to freedom,
She was quiet as a mouse.
Leontyne Price sang opera
And tore down the house!

Constance Baker Motley was a U.S. district judge.
Martin Luther King, Jr. fought for freedom
And wouldn't even budge.
Willie Mays was a baseball superstar.
Patricia Roberts was the first black U.S. ambassador.

W.C. Handy was the father of the blues.
Jan Ernst Matzeliger invented the
First machine to make shoes.
Toni Morrison was a prolific writer.
Fredrick Douglas was a freedom fighter.

Richard Allen was a preacher, an orator.
Mary McLeod Bethune was an educator.
Benjamin Bannecker was an inventor, a poet,
Mathematician, astronomer, a man of peace.
Martin Luther King, Jr. left a legacy
That won't ever cease.

12-20-03

On Attending the Famous Poets' Convention

Poetry took us to another dimension
When we attended the famous poets' convention.
There were people there from all over the world
And we heard an explosion of poetry unfurl.

It didn't matter if you were a layman,
Or had a doctorate degree,
Everyone enjoyed such rich,
Lavish and dramatic poetry.

All the while we were there
They kept our attention
When they took us
To another dimension.

To hear them recite their own invention,
Took us to flight without suspension.
I didn't know before, but now I know it,
The world is full of talented poets.

9-3-02

Section Four: Spiritual Freedom

Cockatiel In a Cage

It is our friend, it is our pet,
But it hasn't found true freedom yet
Betty keeps it locked inside a cage.
Sometimes it rants, sometimes it's in a rage.

Sometimes it sings, sometimes it sighs
We feed it the best food money buys.
But it's not happy, it's not free,
It touched my heart indelibly.

To see it locked inside a cage
It made me rant, it made me rage.
It reminded me of how I use to be,
I once wasn't happy, I once wasn't free.

I had the world and all its pelf
And was in prison inside myself.
Let's free it Betty, let's let it go.
Let's open up its prison door,
Let's open its cage and set it free
Like the Lord has done for you and me.

We are like its parents, it's like our child
But it belongs into the wild.
Let's free it Betty, let's let it soar.
Let's open up its prison door.
Let's open its cage and set it free,
Like the Lord has done for you and me.

Its feathers are glossy, but its body is frail.
The bird reminded me of a man in jail.
Let's free it Betty, Let's let it go.
Let's be its friend and not its foe.
Let's open its cage and let it fly,
Like the Lord has done for you and I.

4-7-01

73

Don't Give Up the Ship

Life sometimes is a pretty bad trip,
But keep sailing, don't give up the ship.
If so, you'll be lost in a sea of sin
Then inflation and cost will engulf you in.

Eventhough our feet are on a firm foundation
Sometimes they have a tendency to slip.
We're often trapped in a perplexed situation,
But keep sailing, don't give up the ship.

Although we're holding onto God's hand
Sometimes we seem to lose our grip,
And we sink into sin like we're in quicksand,
But keep sailing don't give up the ship.

If the ship goes down, go down with the ship
A good captain would stay on board.
You can have utopia at your fingertip
If only you believe in the Lord.

If you must take to the water
Swim or float, don't sink
Because one day soon we'll cross the border
Sooner than we think.

If you give out, don't give up.
One day the ship will sail ashore,
Then happiness will fill your cup
Until your cup will overflow.

4-7-85

Drift away in Music

When I have a problem
And I can't seem to lose it.
I turn on the stereo
And drift away in music.

If a friend does me a favor
And I can't seem to use it.
I turn on the radio
And drift away in music.

Music is a universal language.
It soothes and calms the savage beast,
And if you drift away in music
You can find inner peace.

10-5-80

Calvin Butler

Metamorphosis

People are like worms, tadpoles, and larva
While they are in the world,
But when they find the Lord,
They go through a stage of metamorphosis.
Then like the butterflies, frogs, and flies,
Everything is symmetrically beautiful.
Then we are never worms again.

4-6-90

The Summer is Over

The summer is over, fall is here,
And I can hear rejoicing sounds of cheer.
The heat was exhausting, the rain was wet.
This was indeed a summer, I won't forget.

Yes, the summer is over, fall is here,
But it left me dehydrated, drained and sere.
The weather is changing, the leaves are brown,
And they are gradually falling to the ground.

I wonder how the winter will be.
We can only handle life in a small degree.
I wonder will it be as cold as the summer was wet.
If it does, it will be a winter I won't forget.

After the winter, then comes spring,
And we can hear all the birds as they sing.
The spring represents the beginning of new life.
Then I'll renew my love for my God and my wife.

9-7-03

Calvin Butler

The Winter is Over

Winter is over, spring has sprung
And oh, what a beautiful song is sung.
I hear the birds singing sweetly in the trees.
They sing with the melodious sound of symphonies.

All the birds were singing in harmony and sweet accord
As if they might have been praising the Lord.
The birds sing their songs so beautifully and clear.
It sounds like an anthem that follows after prayer.

A mocking bird was singing alone in a tree.
It sang unorthodoxed , so fitfully.
It doesn't have a song of it's own.
But it sits and sings like a king on a throne.

The mocking bird has a voice that's erratic and strong
And the mocking bird sings all the other birds' songs.
I watched the flowers as their buds unfold
All blue, white, red, yellow, and gold.

They shed their fragrance in the air
Watching God's grandeur makes life easier to bare.
Sometimes I have wintry times in my life,
When I go through trials, tribulations and strife.
But God sends me his creation to comfort my soul
To let me know that He is still in control.

3-10-03

We All Are Equal in the End

We may abuse, we may accuse.
We may misuse and we may offend.
It matters not whether we gain or lose,
We all are equal in the end.

It matters not what nationality.
Nor what color is the skin.
When time comes to face reality,
We all are equal in the end.

We may have different points of view.
We may not always do what we intend.
But when it's time for us to pay our dues,
We all are equal in the end.

When we step on the scale of life
To balance our good against our bad.
Will it be worth the trouble and strife
Or the "good times" we may have had?

It is then we will see for certain
Some of us aren't what we pretend
And what went on behind the closed curtain,
Will be revealed in the end.

9-23-90

Calvin Butler

Aurora

Aurora, Aurora, you're such a beautiful sight,
You are as beautiful as the moon in June,
On a full moon night.
You are as beautiful as the flowers that bloom in the spring.
Aurora, Aurora, you're such a beautiful thing.

T'is you Aurora that breaks the morning
From the pit dark night,
And you Aurora is the dawning
With your beautiful assorted light.

Mere words can't express your beauty
You're something to behold.
I would rather watch your colorful beauty
Than have my weight in gold.

I hope throughout my future years
Your colors keep shining bright,
Then I can shed some joyful tears
For Aurora, my delight.

5-10-80

A Walk Beside the Ocean

My wife and I went for a walk
Beside the Atlantic Ocean.
All at once, we began to talk
About our many notions.

We watched the waves
As they moved to and fro
We found such peace and serenity
Beside the ocean shore.

The waves would come, the waves would go
Without void, without form.
It made us think about how we are
So different from the norm.

The waves would come, the waves would go.
They beckoned after me
And then they washed the sands from the shore
Into another sea.

The waves would come, the waves would go
Like a waiter or a maitre d.'
They really put on a circus show
With such idiosyncrasy.

While the waves would come and go
I really didn't understand
But I left that day from the ocean shore
A wiser and happier man.

Continuous as the waves would come
And beckon after me
I will always love my wife, my confidant
And my friend incessantly.

8-25-90

Life

The union of soul and spirit
Vitality and vim,
Youthful stages and old ages
When your hair turns gray,
And your eyes get dim.

The present, the future, the past
Bad times, blissful times,
Of which we meet unmasked.
A seed, an egg, birth, death, infinity.
Then a contribution to pollution
Just to destroy humanity.

1-7-79

Spontaneous

Life is spontaneous, live it.
Love is spontaneous, give it.
We can control the fact
Whether we tell the truth or a lie
But we can't control the time
When we are born and when we die.

Religion is spontaneous, get it
And if you use an infinitive, don't split it.
We can control the times when we laugh or cry.
But we can't control the times when we live or die.

Micturating is spontaneous, micturate.
Defecating is spontaneous, defecate.
We can control our normenclature.
But we can't control our call to nature.

Justice is spontaneous, serve it.
Respect is spontaneous, if you deserve it
We can control the fact of whether
We tell the truth or a lie
But we can't control the times we laugh or cry.

Aspiring is spontaneous, aspire.
Desiring is spontaneous, desire.
We can control the fact
Whether we tell the truth or a lie
But we can't control the time
When we are born and when we die.

3-7-87

World Peace

One way for us to have world peace
Is for each individual to conquer the beast.
The beast that lives inside each one of us
And resort to a God that we can trust.

Conquer hate, prejudice, and aggression,
Replace it with love and pure obsession.
We could have a peace that would never cease
If ever we learn to conquer the beast.

We could have a love that's pure and strong,
If we could learn to tame our tongue.
We could soar with the eagles, doves, and geese
If we could learn to conquer the beast.

9-11 was a very sad situation
When terrorists brought havoc upon our nation.
I felt like my blood was filled with yeast
But I had to learn to conquer the beast.

Our whole nation was ready to go and fight
But two wrongs don't make a right.
Let's all have a love that want ever cease
Let's all try to conquer the beast.

Section Five: Reverence

A Wreath on the Door

I saw a wreath on a door
Of a family I know
And it was made of holly.
That family use to be happy
But now they are melancholy.

A woman is dead somebody said
And she was warm and human,
And then somebody said, well,
She died a happy woman.

They use to laugh and talk
Under the oak and the loblolly
And down the country road they'd walk
But now they are melancholy.

She left behind her family and friends,
The world and its folly.
Her family might be sad,
But I bet she is jolly.

God Doesn't Hate the Sinner, He only Hates the Sin

God's love for us is like a circle
It has no beginning or an end
God never hates the sinner
He only hates the sin.

We should learn to love our enemy
As much as we love our closet friend
God never hates the sinner.
He only hates the sin.

The devil is God's greatest competitor
And our souls he wants to win
But the devil doesn't love the sinner,
He just loves for us to sin.

Anyone who doesn't know God
Open your heart and let him in
Because God never hates the sinner,
He only hates the sin.

Don't let the devil take you out to dinner
For your soul he'll try to win,
Remember, God doesn't hate the sinner
He only hates the sin.

If you want to be a winner
And you want to make it in,
Let's not ever hate the sinner.
Let's only hate the sin.

In this new millennium
Let's all start a brand new trend.
Let's never hate the sinner
But only hate the sin.

2-2-02

God Is Already Here

God is already here, take a look around
He's the sunlight in our hair,
He's our shadow on the ground.
He's the whisper in the wind
He's our invisible friend.
I know that God really cares,
I can feel Him in my prayer.
Because He's already here.
God is already here,
Let me try to explain.
He's the warm gentle sunlight,
He's the cool refreshing rain.
He's that whisper in the wind,
He's our invisible friend.
I know that God really cares.
I can feel Him in my prayer.
Because He's already here.
God is already here!
I wonder have you heard
How He takes care of everything
Even the little bird.
He's that whisper in the wind,

He's our invisible friend.
I know that God really cares,
I can feel Him in my prayer,
Because He's already here.
God is already here!
He is very vast.
He is the sunlight in our hair.
He's the dew that's on the grass.
He's that whisper in the wind.
He can be your enemy or your friend.
I know God really cares.
I can feel him in my prayer.
Because He's already here!
God is already here.

Does this sound absurd?
Well, He's doing everything
That He said in His word.
He's that whisper in the wind.
He will be with us until the end.
I know that God really cares.
I can feel Him in my prayer.
Because He's already here.
God is already here!
Can't you hear the sound
Of His music in the air
And feel His blessings coming down?
He's that whisper in the wind,
He's our invisible friend.
I know that God really cares.
Can you feel Him in your prayer?
God is already here.

8-25-02

I Believe That There's a God Somewhere

I believe that there's a God somewhere
I can feel his presence in the atmosphere.
Eventhough I've never seen his glorious face
I can always feel his redeeming grace.
There's a God somewhere.

I believe that there's a God somewhere
Who will always answer an honest prayer
For if you pray and you are sincere,
He will always lend a listening ear.
There's a God somewhere.

I believe that there's a God somewhere
Who will never leave us in despair.
When I was down and out, didn't have a friend
And had been tossed about like sand in the wind

He was the only one that came to my rescue.
Now He's the only one that I pursue.
There's a God somewhere.

2-9-87

Section Six: Supernatural Mysteries

Apparition of a Dead Man

Long ago in the days of yore,
While I was but a child,
There lived a man with power in his hand.
In the swamps where the trees grew wild.

If ever I'd go near, weird noises I'd hear.
The lightning clashed, the thunder roared,
And on the floor the mice would crawl,
The windows flew open, and so did the doors,
As he cast his image on the wall.

The wicked man died but he clarified,
"I'll be back to haunt the land,"
And you know I dread everything he said,
His least wish is my greatest command.

I thought through suspicion, not as an apparition,
But by reincarnation, he might live again.
But without feet or head, he came back from the dead,
With magical powers in his hand.

When he I beheld, my blood ran cold.
He scared me out of my wits.
The hair stood on my head, I was so afraid.
He tore my courage into little bits.

Through death and infinity, he came to this vicinity,
To terrorize humanity,
He I detest, he is a pest,
It's hard to keep my sanity.

As I go about my task, people always ask,
"Is it fact or superstition?"
All I have to say in a meaningful way,
I saw a dead man's apparition.
3-24-69

Histories Mysteries

Once upon a time in history
Our nation created a major mystery,
Making war against our neighbors
Far beyond our nation's shore.
.

But while they nodded nearly sleeping
Terrorists came a creeping, came a creeping
With fear and anthrax slowly seeping,
Seeping into our nation's core.

I wonder what was their reason.
Was it hatred or an act of treason?
Those terrorists came alarming,
Methodically bombing, methodically bombing,
The Pentagon and the World Trade Center
In New York and Washington, D.C. about a month ago.

Isn't Bin Laden our neighbor, our brother?
But he's like no other,
But didn't the same God create him
That created us, the God we all adore?

Will we live to see tomorrow?
Through this terror, through this horror,
All this killing, no remorse, and no sorrow.
Tell me truly, I implore.

But Osama Bin Laden, never yielding,
Still is zealing, still is zealing,
For his cause, for his country
To win a war he's fought before.

When our nation was severely saddened
By a man named Osama Bin Laden,
President Bush pledged to bring justice
To our nation we all adore.

He asked the Taliban to submit him
And don't acquit him
Quotes: the Taliban "Nevermore!"
Master mind Bin Laden,
Is he satan? Is he satan?

Or is he one of God's angels
Fighting for a God we all adore?
Will our nation win the war
Against Afghanistan and the Taliban?
Quotes: Bin Laden "Nevermore!"

Deep into the mountains peering,
Soldiers stand there, wondering, fearing,
Doubting, dreaming dreams no Americans
Ever dared to dream before.

Back into the mountains turning
Bin Laden's passions within him burning,
All his passions within him yearning
Osama Bin Laden wants to win a war,
Against the super power nation
That's never been won before.

Is Bin Laden a prophet or a devil?
Is he an angel or a man of evil?
Was he meant to rise above us?
Tell me truly, I implore!
Can we win this war against terrorism?
Other wars have been won before.
Quotes: Bin Laden "Nevermore."

Bin Laden's hijackers caused chaos and panic
They took more lives than Pearl Harbor
And the Titanic.
Was this an act of God
Or was it satanic?
Tell me truly, I implore!

Because of an act of self-exaltation
God may have turned away from our nation,
And allowed our enemies to conquer us
In a way we never imagined before.

All this hatred, all this killing
Leaves me with an empty feeling
Somewhat remorseful, somewhat chilling.
Will our nation ever exonerate itself
As it once was before
Quotes: Bin Laden "Nevermore."

Bin Laden reminds me of the "Raven"
He's always quoted as misbehaving
He is to President Bush what the "raven"
Was to Edgar Allen Poe.

Prophet said I, if man of evil,
Prophet still if fiend or devil
Will our nation be acquitted ever?
Tell me truly, I implore!

Were the bombings a lesson or a blessing?
Or was it compulsive political obsession?
Will our nation come closer together
Closer than we were before?

Will Osama Bin Laden
That was never sadden, never sadden
Apologize to our nation?
Quotes: Bin Laden "Nevermore!"

Is this because of Desert Storm?
Kuwait or Vietnam?
Can we ever find any healing balm?
Tell me truly, I implore.

They say, Peace in the Middle East."
When all the fighting won't ever cease.
Americans, are we domestic?
Or are we the beast?
Quotes the poet "I don't know."

10-31-01

The Bottomless Pit

Once while sleeping in my bed
Visions of demons danced over my head.
They took me to a world of dread
Where angels would dare not tread.

They threw me in a bottomless pit
I kept falling, falling, I never quit.
Falling until the water, I hit
Which was in the bottomless pit.

I asked a ghoul, "Are you the devil?"
But he ignored me and answered, "Never."
And the only thing was spoken ever
Was "You're lost in a valley of sin."

I fell through dimensions of the past,
Ghouls and ghosts, I met aghast,
Who followed fast and followed fast
On a chase that had no end.

Then I fell through slush and slime
All the way back to my origin of time,
Through muck, mush, and grime,
Until once again I was in my prime.

I was petrified one hair from dying,
All my fears kept multiplying.
I asked the Lord in agony, crying,
"Rid me of this weird place?"

He said, "It all was just a dream,"
But reality to me it seemed,
And every ray and every beam,
Shown on a horrifying face.

Weightlessly I floated through space,
Bats and vampires followed with haste.
There wasn't any gravity any place,
And the smell of dead perfumed the air.

Then the air grew sweet and mild,
And I stopped to reminisce for a while.
Suddenly I felt so infantile.
Then I awakened from a terrible nightmare.

5-29-75

About The Author

Calvin Butler lives in Trenton, South Carolina. He loves writing poetry, but also reading and listening to the poetry of others. Many of his poems are written to his wife. A few have been included. He also writes inspirational, tributes, and mystery poems. His title *Coming Out of My Shell* is appropriate because he used to be extremely timid and would never think of sharing his poetry with others until friends discovered his talent and encouraged him to share and eventually have his poems published.

www.ingramcontent.com/pod-product-compliance
Lightning Source LLC
Chambersburg PA
CBHW051447280526
45785CB00003B/1468